16-9

ROBERT O. HOFFELT

HOW
TO LEAD
INFORMAL
SINGING

ABINGDON ✠ PRESS

NEW YORK — NASHVILLE

HOW TO LEAD INFORMAL SINGING

SET UP, PRINTED, AND BOUND BY
THE PARTHENON PRESS, AT NASHVILLE,
TENNESSEE, UNITED STATES OF AMERICA

PREFACE

During recent years there has been a steady and healthy revival of interest in group singing. The value of singing together for purposes of fun, fellowship, recreation, worship, motivation, therapy, and the like, is recognized as an established fact.

Since a group of people seldom can just start singing songs well together, and keep at it enthusiastically, one of the big problems that has been obvious in this renewed and growing interest in group singing is the task of finding and/or training capable leaders. This has not been easy. (Paradoxically, even excellent choral and instrumental conductors many times are not effective song leaders.) While no amount of words and diagrams printed in a book can guarantee that a person will become an effective song leader, this book attempts to set forth some of the basic techniques and ideas necessary among the skills of such a leader.

There probably are as many ways and "methods" of conducting as there are conductors in the professional music field. The same may be said of song leaders. Experienced song leaders have their own pet theories of how best to lead group singing, and ex-

3

cellent results may be achieved from a variety of approaches. Therefore, the suggestions, beat patterns, and ideas given herein are presented as *a way,* and certainly are not to be thought of as the *only* way. They are based, however, upon many years of study and experience and are known to be successful when used properly.

This book is not in any sense a text on the techniques of choral conducting. Examination will reveal, though, that there is much included in these pages that should benefit a serious student of conducting.

The primary purpose of this book is to inform and instruct prospective song leaders. In addition, the author hopes it (1) will serve to stimulate further interest in group singing in general, (2) will present ways and means of heightening both individual and collective satisfaction and enjoyment from singing together, (3) will encourage the use of the highest type songs in the best way possible for dynamic group activity, and (4) will help motivate serious-minded individuals to study further and appreciate the whole realm of music. To these ends are these pages dedicated.

ROBERT O. HOFFELT

CONTENTS

CHAPTER I

General Observations

Anyone with a sense of rhythm can learn to lead group singing. Naturally, the more experience one has had in music in general the easier and quicker the mechanics of song leading are acquired. However, it is a common mistake (more common among musicians, incidentally) to believe that the only people qualified to lead songs effectively are those who have a strong music education.

A good rhythmic sense is important, however. Most people can develop this rhythmic sensitivity through well-guided musical experiences; it doesn't take a great artist to "find and feel the beat." (Even savages instinctively give the right accents in their primitive rhythms.) The ability to recognize and feel the accent, then, is of prime importance to the beginning song leader. But it is not enough for the leader alone to feel rhythm; the necessity of stimulating this rhythmic response in the singers should be obvious if the song session is to be successful.

A fine solo voice is not essential for effective song leading. Many of the best song leaders in the country would fail miserably if they had to depend upon their abilities as solo artists! A clear and pleasing quality to one's voice *is* a very real asset though. It is difficult to be authoritative and inspire enthusiasm with a voice that is husky, colorless, weak, or lacks projection. Where real vocal problems exist, the aspiring song leader might do well to take some voice lessons or coaching from a qualified teacher; if the difficulty is from a physical condition, medical attention, of course, is advisable. While most people can improve their voices by intelligent study and practice, clarity and pleasant quality of the voice are inherent in a great many people. They need only to become accustomed to using their voices, and such study is not at all necessary for effective song leading.

A pleasant personality and enthusiasm are essential for effective song leading. There are no substitutes for these qualities in a song leader. No amount of mere technical knowledge and perfection will ever take the place of a smile, of personal magnetism, charm, and enthusiasm in song leading. If singers *like* their song leader and are drawn to him by his own affability and geniality, they will respond far better than if they instinctively react passively, or even negatively, to him.

This does not imply that an artificial attitude of any sort should be developed or displayed by song leaders —not at all; singers are quick to recognize a lack of sincerity on the part of a leader. Beginning song leaders should try to develop true love of people, a genuine appreciation for both individual and group personalities, and real zeal for the opportunity at hand to utilize the powers of music in group activity.

This personal magnetism of a song leader should make his people want to sing just for the fun of singing, and should so draw them to him that they are truly sorry when the song session is over. There is nothing that satisfies a leader quite so much after such a session as to have people cluster around him brimful of happiness and excitement demanding more of the same type of fare!

Being constantly alert certainly is a part of personality and enthusiasm. An alert leader will seize opportunities as they appear to heighten the interest during a time of singing. These might present themselves in a variety of ways. Even such things as the current temperature or weather conditions, the lights suddenly going out, boys all sitting together, latecomers, a sticking key, or dead notes on the piano can be turned into moments of excitement and fun by an alert director. Also, this alertness certainly should manifest itself *before* the time of singing; an alert leader can recognize possible opportunities to heighten interest even as he plans his song session.

Good song leading involves the use of gestures that are simple, clear, decisive, and expressive. In addition,

9

outstanding directors are also inspirational and artistic.

Simplicity in directing is exactly what the term implies: there is no need for a person to use fancy and elaborate gestures that are meaningless in themselves. Wild gesticulation and mere waving of the arms, even though they be rhythmic in nature, are not conducive to getting a satisfying response from a group.

Clarity of gestures involves simplicity, but in addition demands precision and organization. There should never be a question as to where the "downbeat" is. A certain amount of routine motion of the hands necessarily will result in gaining both a simple and clear style, but that is a virtue rather than a liability. A director of singing should never be uncertain as to which direction his next beat should go, or what type of gesture he should use. Automatic reflexes which come as a result of routine time-beating are, as we will see later, an asset to a conductor.

Decisiveness in directing leaves no doubt in the minds of the singers as to the type of response desired. This is a matter of exactitude, of being entirely in command of the situation, of well-executed beat patterns, with no ambiguous motions that call attention only to themselves without any real purpose as far as group response is concerned. Likewise, the gestures must not be mousy or timid in character. Decisiveness is the element which gives authority to

10

conducting gestures; it is the quality of true leadership in terms of specific visible motions.

Expressive song leading seeks to reflect the spirit of the music in the style of beat used. In turn, the style of the beat will determine the style of musical response from the singers. Obviously, a quiet and contemplative song would call for rather small and subdued beat-patterns, whereas a rollicking and spirited song would demand larger and more vigorous gestures. Smooth and flowing beat patterns would be used for legato passages, and an angular and forceful style for strongly accented and marcato passages.

In addition to simplicity, clarity, decisiveness, and being expressive, the finest song leaders are certainly inspiring. They themselves will have had to be inspired by the music they seek to present and by the opportunities they discover as they actually present that music at a specific occasion. But it isn't enough for a director alone to be inspired if he is to be a superior leader. His manner, style, musicianship, personality, enthusiasm, originality, background and training, intelligence, and character all combine in a mighty invisible force that inspires his singers and evokes a real emotional response from them. This ability to be inspiring cannot be taught; it cannot be developed by mere routine practicing. It must come through growth, through leadership training and ability, through experience, through maturity of

11

judgment, and other such recognizable but elusive attributes. It must be striven for, but it cannot be attained in just the same manner as perfection is reached in an ordinary skill.

Artistry also is not easily defined or attained. This involves depth of understanding, breadth of living, degree of emotional maturity, and other intangible qualities that will differ greatly in individuals. Artistry rightfully has been termed a "spark of The Divine." In a sense it is the outward manifestation of inner convictions regarding beauty and truth. It is the overall manner of releasing in an ethereal way the very concrete and valid emotions which lie deep in the soul of man. It may even involve a sense of the dramatic, but not the theatrical; these terms are not synonymous and must not be confused. To be dramatic is to seize upon the opportunities presented by the forces at hand and the situation of the moment in order to portray sincerely a truth, present an idea, or achieve an emotional response in the finest and best and often the quickest way possible. The song leader who has this quality of artistry is a gem; he strives constantly for the perfection that he himself feels and experiences deep within himself, but he is never completely satisfied or happy with the results of his efforts.

Much has been said thus far about gestures, or beat patterns. They are extremely important in successful song leading, and most of the early training of conductors of necessity involves a lengthy period of training while learning these patterns. However, the actual beat pattern itself is *not* the most important element to keep foremost in mind while leading songs. The most important thing a director of informal singing must remember is *to make these musical ex*: *periences enjoyable and to utilize all the potential possible to be found in the music for fun, fellowship, worship, or for whatever other purpose exists at the moment.* This just cannot be stressed too much in the matter of leading group singing.

A professional conductor, who is a conductor in *every* sense of the word—symphonic, choral, band— rightfully and properly will have other elements which he considers of prime importance. Among these will be technical accuracy, balance, blend, intonation, interpretation, style, emotion, just to name a few. But the song leader is concerned about such items as these only from a secondary standpoint. He is far more interested in the *people* under his direction, and their personal response to the music, than he is in the proper and convincing performance of a great work of music. Interestingly enough, though, some of our most effective song leaders are also the finest conductors of serious professional and semi-professional performing groups. A logical observation is that these top-notch song leaders who are known also as successful and authoritative conductors in other fields recognize wherein the emphasis should be placed in these utterly different situations; they intelligently approach each in its own manner.

Further, as intimated earlier, the better the musician and the more experience he has had in music, both as a performer and a listener, the easier it will be for him to be a successful song leader. Self-confidence, poise, accuracy, and just plain effectiveness will be forthcoming quicker and easier with a good musical background. However, that in no way obscures or nullifies our first observation: *anyone* with a sense of rhythm can learn to lead songs!

CHAPTER II

Basic Beat Patterns

How to practice beat patterns to gain simplicity, clarity, and decisiveness: Study all this section carefully before attempting the beat patterns. This is important!

Whenever possible practice the beat patterns while standing before a mirror. This will enable you to see yourself as others will see you, will assist you in developing good habits while conducting, and will help you to avoid forming distracting mannerisms. Stand with good posture: feet comfortably placed, somewhat apart with one foot a little in front of the other, heels slightly turned in so you have good balance; let your lower abdomen be drawn in and your chest high with shoulders back—not rigidly so, but just comfortably erect. Your posture should give you a feeling of security and well-being; it should give your singers a feeling of confidence in you—a sense that you are completely in command of the situation at hand and therefore worthy of their attention, respect, and cooperation. Practice often enough and long enough before the mirror with good posture until your stance and countenance become habitual and you lose your self-consciousness.

15

Before actually describing the beat patterns that follow, here is a little device that may seem senseless but will enhance your conducting and ultimately shorten your practice time. Imagine you are bouncing a rubber ball. "Bounce" it steadily, but occasionally change the force of it: bounce it vigorously; now with moderation; now vigorously again; now very easily. The reason for doing this is that the beat patterns do have a bouncy characteristic at just the precise moment of each beat. This bounce is referred to variously as "rebound," "wristflick," "beat-point," "ictus," "click," or "takt" (recurring bounce).

The wrist should be loose and flexible, but not floppy, while "bouncing the ball." Let the elbow and forearm be away from the body; use the forearm in conjunction with the wrist for a graceful motion in bouncing the imaginary ball *exactly straight up and down*. The palm of the hand should be down, although neither it nor the fingers should be held stiffly; both should feel loose, but under control and certainly not flimsy.

When the "bouncing ball" has been practiced so that it appears natural and graceful in front of the mirror, you are ready to try the beat patterns. In these early stages do not use music; it will only distract you. A metronome will help to keep a steady tempo, but is not at all necessary. Simply describe the particular patterns in front of the mirror until they feel free and easy and look like the diagram. Still retain the bouncy characteristic in the pattern that you developed with the imaginary rubber ball; later on the style of the music itself will determine how much bounce you will retain in your style of beat. Stick with one beat pattern long enough to master it thoroughly before going on to the next. When you stand before a group, you cannot be conscious of the direction in which your hand should be moving or how it should look; therefore, the beat patterns must be practiced until they become habitual and automatic.

These beat patterns must be executed with great care and precision. "Any old way" just won't do; exactness has no substitute at this stage of your learning. Later, after you have had experience, you may want to deviate from these basic diagrams, and you will then be able to do so with ease and authority, but not now.

Do not attempt fancy flourishes and wild flailing of the arms. Neither should the patterns be mousy; for practice purposes describe a bold sort of beat approximately the distance from shoulder to waist. You will want to change this later on according to the style music you will be conducting. The rebound should not be more than half the size of the downbeat for each pattern.

After a basic beat pattern has been learned and practiced thoroughly, and only then, should you proceed to beat time to music. Then utilize recordings, radio, TV, someone else playing the piano or singing, and any other method to gain experience beating time to actual music.

Only those patterns are included that ordinarily are encountered in leading the usual types of songs for group singing.

Note: The patterns given are for right-handed persons using the right hand. Although professional conductors invariably do use the right hand for the beat patterns, there is no reason why a *song leader* who is left-handed should not beat time with his left hand. In this case, simply reverse the *left* and *right* directions.

The Two-Beat Pattern

Use this beat pattern for songs with the following time-signatures:

$\frac{2}{4}$ $\frac{2}{2}$ $\math₵$, $\frac{2}{8}$, fast $\frac{4}{4}$ C, and lively $\frac{6}{8}$ or $\frac{6}{4}$.

The basic directions of the hand are *down, up.*

Fig. 1

18

The actual beat pattern resembles a fishhook:

FIG. 2

The shaded area indicates the impact of the beat itself; this is the "bounce," the rebound, or ictus. It is a flicking motion of the whole hand.

Keep the palm down, elbow and forearm somewhat raised and out to the side, wrist and fingers flexible, but not flimsy. Left hand should remain at the side. Practice without music until the beat pattern feels and looks comfortable, natural, and graceful.

The two-beat pattern is used for directing songs like the following:

$\frac{2}{4}$ Row, Row, Row Your Boat
Oh! Susanna
Li'l Liza Jane
Dixie
When You Wore a Tulip

19

$\frac{2}{2}$ ¢   Over the Rainbow
            Anchors Aweigh
            The Caissons Go Rolling Along

$\frac{4}{4}$ C   Alouette
(*lively*)   Polly Wolly Doodle
            Deck the Hall

$\frac{6}{8}$ (*lively*)   For He's a Jolly Good Fellow
            The More We Get Together
            Sailing
            Good-Bye, My Lover, Good-Bye

$\frac{6}{4}$ (*lively*)   Jesus Loves Even Me

Note: It is better not to beat songs in lively $\frac{4}{4}$ $\frac{6}{8}$ and $\frac{6}{4}$ in "two" unless your group knows them well and can sing them up to tempo.

The Three-Beat Pattern

Use this beat pattern for songs with the following time-signatures: $\frac{3}{4}$ $\frac{3}{2}$ $\frac{3}{8}$, and lively $\frac{9}{8}$.

The basic directions of the hand are *down, right, up:*

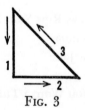

Fig. 3

20

Utilizing the "bounce" for the actual impact of the beat, the pattern becomes as fellows:

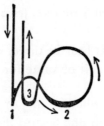

FIG. 4

Notice that the second beat is rounded like a circle.

Drill: Practice the following changes of patterns: 2 2 3 3 2 2 3 3 2 2 3 3 2 2 3 3 etc. (*Optional:* Set metronome at $\quad = 100$)
2 3 2 3 2 3 2 3 2 3 2 3 2 3 2 3 etc.

The three-beat pattern is used for directing songs and hymns like the following:

$\frac{3}{4}$ My Country, 'Tis of Thee
The Star-Spangled Banner
Happy Birthday to You
Home on the Range
My Bonnie

$\frac{3}{2}$ Rock of Ages, Cleft for Me
Jesus Calls Us

21

* $\frac{3}{8}$ We Three Kings of Orient Are
  Sweet Hour of Prayer

$\frac{9}{8}$ Blessed Assurance, Jesus Is Mine!

Note: When $\frac{9}{8}$ is beat in three, the dotted quarter note (♩.) is the unit of value for each beat.

* Lively songs, whether in $\frac{3}{4}$ or $\frac{3}{8}$, sometimes are better directed with *one* beat to the measure. This is simply a down-up motion like the bouncing rubber ball as practiced on page 16. This motion is as follows:

Fig. 5

The Four-Beat Pattern

Use this beat pattern for songs with the following time-signatures: $\frac{4}{4}$ C, $\frac{4}{2}$, and $\frac{4}{8}$ (not commonly found).

22

The basic directions of the hand are *down, left, right, up.*

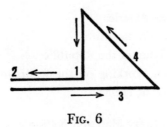

FIG. 6

The actual beat pattern is as follows:

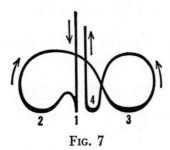

FIG. 7

The rounded second and third beats give a graceful character to this pattern.

Drill: Practice the following changes of patterns:

♩=112

```
2 2 3 3 4 4 2 2 3 3 4 4 2 2 3 3 4 4
2 3 4 4 3 2 3 4 4 3 2 3 4 4 3 2 3 4
2 4 3 4 2 4 3 4 2 4 3 4 2 4 3 4 2 4
```

23

The four-beat pattern is used for directing songs and hymns like the following:

$\frac{4}{4}$ God Bless America
America, the Beautiful
Battle Hymn of the Republic
I've Been Working on the Railroad
Old Folks at Home

$\frac{4}{2}$ Once to Every Man and Nation
Dear Lord and Father of Mankind
Jesus, Lover of My Soul (*Tune:* Aberystwyth)
O Love That Wilt Not Let Me Go

Note: Lively songs in $\frac{4}{4}$ may be directed better in "two"; see pages 18-20.

The Six-Beat Pattern

Use this beat pattern for songs with the following time signatures: $\frac{6}{8}$ (slow) and $\frac{6}{4}$.

The basic directions of the hand are *down, left, left, right, right, up.*

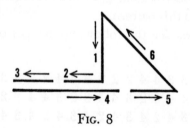

Fig. 8

The actual beat pattern is as follows:

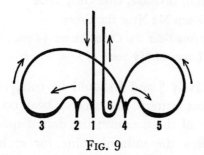

Fig. 9

Be careful not to turn the palm and wrist up when crossing to the fourth beat of the pattern.

Drill: Practice the following changes of patterns:

♩=120

```
6 6 4 4 6 6 3 3 6 6 2 2 6 6 4 4 6
6 2 6 3 6 4 6 2 6 3 6 4 6 2 6 3
2 4 3 6 6 2 4 3 6 6 2 4 3 6 6
6 4 3 2 6 4 3 2 6 4 3 2 6 4 3 2
```

The six-beat pattern is used for directing songs and hymns like the following:

$\frac{6}{8}$ Drink to Me Only With Thine Eyes
  Silent Night
  It Came Upon the Midnight Clear
  Softly and Tenderly Jesus is Calling

25

$\frac{6}{4}$ Day Is Dying in the West

Immortal, Invisible, God Only Wise

Jesus, Keep Me Near the Cross

Must Jesus Bear the Cross Alone (*Tune:* Maitland)

Jesus, Lover of My Soul (*Tune:* Martyn)

Note: Lively $\frac{6}{8}$ and $\frac{6}{4}$ should be conducted using the *two*-beat pattern, the second beat occuring on count four of the measure; the dotted quarter note (♩.) is then the unit of value for each beat in $\frac{6}{8}$, and the dotted half note (♩.) in $\frac{6}{4}$.

The "Panic" Pattern

If the truth were known, even the best of conductors may "lose the beat" sometimes. When that happens it is necessary to continue beating time without a definite pattern until the established beat pattern can be found again; the song leader must not stop his directing or even hesitate!

The following diagram shows a motion of the hand that will suffice perfectly well during those moments when you are without the regular pattern. It is a curved, rocking motion that works for any rhythmic scheme:

FIG. 10

This device may be continued almost indefinitely without a downbeat until you "find" a place for the downbeat and can get back into your regular pattern.

Or at times the downbeat can be felt, but the other beats in the pattern may be elusive. In this case the "panic" pattern is thus:

FIG. 11

Repeat this as long as necessary until the true pattern is established again. The downbeat is always on count "one" of the measure, and the rocking motion continues for each of the other counts. It really doesn't matter in which direction the rocking motion begins or ends; either to the left or right works equally well.

This "panic" beat pattern *must not* be considered an all-time sufficient substitute for the legitimate beat pattern. It is for emergency use only, and is *not* in any sense an alternate pattern.

27

CHAPTER III

The Preparatory Beat

A group must have a signal to begin singing; they cannot "just start." This signal may be given verbally or in the form of a gesture, or both. This is similar to the method of giving military commands such as "Forward, March!" or "Right, Face!"; the first word of such a command acts for the military group just as the preparatory beat does for singers.

The preparatory beat, or preliminary beat, commonly is referred to as the "upbeat." There are two types: that which is given when the song begins on a whole count, and that which is given when the song begins on a partial count. Figure 12 illustrates the former, that is, a song beginning on a whole count.

Row, row, row your boat

Fig. 12

This whole count need not be the first beat of the measure; it can occur on any beat. Figure 13 illustrates a song beginning on a partial count.

The sun shines bright in the old Ken-tuck-y home,

Fig. 13

It is conceivable that this partial count may be from any beat in the measure, not necessarily the last.

Beginning on a Whole Count

When a song begins on a full count, regardless of which one, a gesture will need to be given in the *same tempo* and style as occuring in the beat pattern that follows. This is important. A slow, leisurely sort of gesture would not precede a vigorous pattern that follows. Likewise, a fast motion would not precede a more deliberate pattern. This preparatory gesture must agree with the type of beat pattern to be used.

There are several kinds of gestures which may be used, but perhaps the easiest for beginners would be an inward and upward motion, such as the following:

Fig. 14

Later on you may wish to vary this preliminary motion. When the words "Ready, sing!" are used (or something similar) this motion is given on the word "sing."

For songs beginning on the first count of the measure, the preparatory beat and first beat are as follows:

29

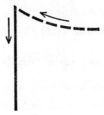

FIG. 15

Practice this motion over and over again using all the beat patterns.

Examples:

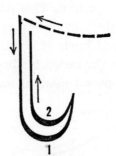

FIG. 16

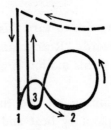

FIG. 17

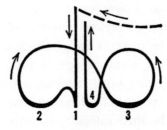

Fig. 18

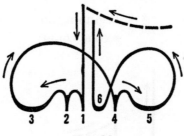

Fig. 19

Remember, this inward and upward preliminary swing that forms the preparatory beat must be in the same tempo as the beats that follow.

This same inward and upward motion is used as the preparatory beat for any song that begins *on a count* other than the first. As long as the first note comprises an entire count, regardless of which it happens to be in the measure, this same preparatory beat can be used—and then the regular *remaining* beats of the pattern are used.

31

Following are examples of preparatory beats for songs beginning on various counts, then the remaining beats of the patterns are given. Study these carefully. They may seem strange at first, but practice each one diligently until it seems natural and easy. If you know your basic beat patterns thoroughly, there should be little difficulty in mastering this important phase of conducting.

$\frac{2}{2}$ $\frac{2}{4}$ beginning on
second count:

Up, my neigh-bor, come a-way,

FIG. 20

$\frac{3}{2}$ $\frac{3}{8}$ $\frac{3}{4}$ beginning on
second count:
(not common)

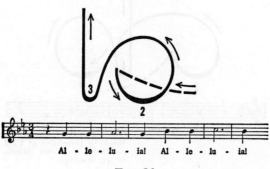

FIG. 21

$\frac{3}{2}$ $\frac{3}{8}$ $\frac{3}{4}$ beginning on
third count:

FIG. 22

33

$\frac{4}{2}$ $\frac{4}{8}$ $\frac{4}{4}$ beginning on
second count:

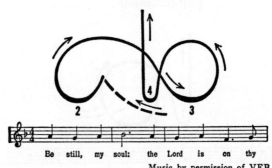

Be still, my soul: the Lord is on thy

Music by permission of VEB
Breitkopf & Hartel Musik-
verlag, Leipzig.

FIG. 23

$\frac{4}{2}$ $\frac{4}{8}$ $\frac{4}{4}$ beginning on
third count:

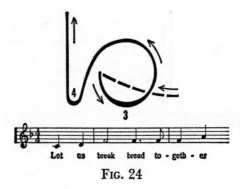

Let us break bread to - geth - er

FIG. 24

$\begin{smallmatrix}4\\2\end{smallmatrix}$ $\begin{smallmatrix}4\\8\end{smallmatrix}$ $\begin{smallmatrix}4\\4\end{smallmatrix}$ beginning on
fourth count:

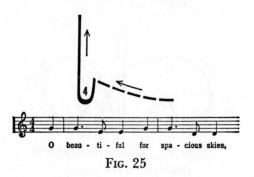

O beau - ti - ful for spa - cious skies,

FIG. 25

$\begin{smallmatrix}6\\8\end{smallmatrix}$ $\begin{smallmatrix}6\\4\end{smallmatrix}$ beginning on
second count:

(rare)

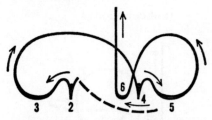

(Included for information and
drill purposes only.)

FIG. 26

35

$\begin{smallmatrix} 6 \\ 8 \end{smallmatrix}$ $\begin{smallmatrix} 6 \\ 4 \end{smallmatrix}$ beginning on
third count:

(rare)

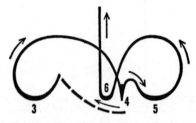

(Included for information and
drill purposes only.)

FIG. 27

$\begin{smallmatrix} 6 \\ 8 \end{smallmatrix}$ $\begin{smallmatrix} 6 \\ 4 \end{smallmatrix}$ beginning on
fourth count:

(not common)

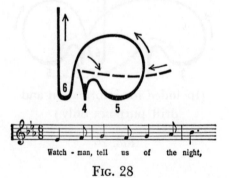

Watch - man, tell us of the night,

FIG. 28

6 6 beginning on
8 4 fifth count:

(rare)

Oh, Ma - rie,____ oh, Ma - rie____

FIG. 29

6 6 beginning on
8 4 sixth count:

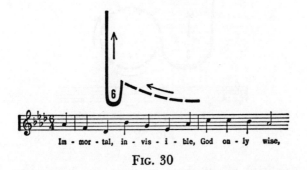

Im - mor - tal, in - vis - i - ble, God on - ly wise,

FIG. 30

37

When giving a preparatory beat for a song beginning on a full count, some song leaders prefer to reverse the direction from that in the preceding diagrams, so that the motion is *outward* and *upward,* in
this manner:

FIG. 31

Still others simply give the *preceding* full beat without any preliminary inward *or* outward motion. Thus,
a song in $\frac{3}{4}$ beginning on the third count would be
indicated as follows:

The ash - grove, how — grace - ful,

FIG. 32

Any and all of these motions are legitimate; it
doesn't matter too much what the motion actually is

38

as long as it is positively there, and in the style and tempo of the beats that follow.

Beginning on a Partial Count

When a song begins on a partial count (see Fig. 13), regardless of which count it happens to be in the measure, simply give that full beat as the preparatory beat without the preceding preliminary motion. When "Ready, Sing!" is used, the hand is motionless on the word "Ready" and then executes that complete beat on the word "Sing." The complete beat should be somewhat larger in order to insure a smooth entrance. Example:

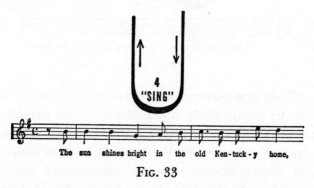

The sun shines bright in the old Ken-tuck-y home,

FIG. 33

Since it is difficult, if not impossible, for any group to "divide" a beat properly for a smooth entrance without considerable rehearsal, some directors prefer to give the entire and complete preceding beat *as well as the full beat* where the entrance is to be made

39

as preparatory motions. In this instance, when "Ready, Sing!" is used, the hand describes the complete preceding beat on "Ready," using a somewhat smaller motion than usual, and then gives the beat for the entrance in a larger manner with the word "Sing."

Example:

A Span - ish Cav - a - lier   stood in   his re - treat,

FIG. 34

While preliminary beats may seem confusing at first, by careful study of the directions and examples given and with diligent practice they should become easy to handle. In fact, they must become so natural and matter-of-course that the song leader should never have to stop and think what he should do to start his group singing exactly together.

40

CHAPTER IV

The Fermata and the Release

The fermata $(\frown)$, is referred to variously as a "hold" or "bird's-eye." It brings about a momentary stoppage of the flow of rhythm and therefore *also the beat pattern*. There is no rule that regulates how long a fermata should be held; this is left to the artistry and discretion of the conductor.

In songs that are used for group singing the fermata may be found over a note or rest of any value.

When the fermata occurs, the hand no longer continues the beat pattern; it remains suspended in midair, but preferably it keeps moving slightly during this time. This movement of the hand, be it ever so small and without direction or pattern, serves to retain the attention of the group. It also implies the continuation of the larger meter of the phrase, even though rhythmic pulsation within the measure ceases momentarily. This movement might look something like the following, with the fermata occuring on the third beat as an example:

41

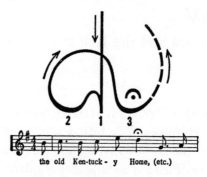

FIG. 35

A similar type of movement is desirable when the fermata occurs on any other beat in the measure. The direction taken by the hand and character of this movement will come naturally to the song leader as a result of such things as style of the song, tempo, dynamic level, size of the group and, to some extent, the beat of the measure containing the fermata. It may be safe to assume that the general direction of such movement will be toward the next beat that follows.

Sometimes it is necessary to accentuate this motion for a fermata by intensifying or enlarging the suspended position of the hand, or doing so with both hands. And occasionally a director may find it necessary to sing quite strongly himself at that point or even admonish the group to "WATCH!" in order to keep them together.

42

To continue beat patterns after observing a fermata there are two considerations:

1. *When the words continue without a break in the phrase* return immediately to the next regular beat that follows. Possibly that beat should be accentuated somewhat so your singers will move exactly with you and there can be no question in their minds when to resume the phrase.

Example:

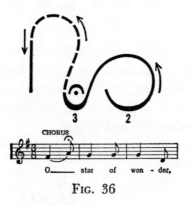

FIG. 36

2. *When the fermata is followed by a break in the words* (i.e., at the end of a phrase or between two independent grammatical phrases), *or when the music itself unmistakably calls for a definite break,* it will be necessary to give a gesture for the release (see page 45).

43

Example:

bring   back,   Oh,   bring   back   my

FIG. 37

When this release is given *in the rhythm and tempo* of the song (or phrase), the gesture itself serves as the preliminary beat for the group to begin the next phrase. This is important for the beginning song leader to understand and master.

Example of the gesture for release serving as a preliminary beat:

bring   back,   Oh,   bring   back   my

FIG. 38

44

If for some reason the gesture for release is *not* given in the same rhythm and tempo of the phrase, or if a pause follows the release, a regular preparatory beat will need to be given for all to begin singing together (see page 29).

Note: When the fermata occurs on a note receiving more than one count, or in syncopation, it is not necessary to indicate each count in the beat pattern. It is necessary, however, to sustain the note for a longer time than the basic value of the note.

Examples:

FIG. 39

There are various motions that may be given which will serve as a cutoff so the group will stop together. Perhaps one of the simplest and most effective, and most graceful, is the act of describing a loop:

FIG. 40

The shaded area indicates where the exact moment of cutoff occurs. This gesture is given with snap of the wrist and forearm, and should be definite and graceful. A word of caution: Never let it appear flippant or unimportant; in effective song leading stopping together is just as important as starting together. The gesture for release may be given easily after any beat in any beat pattern.

Examples:

After two in the two-beat pattern

FIG. 41

After two in the three-beat pattern

FIG. 42

After two in the four-beat pattern
(also six-beat pattern)

FIG. 43

After three in the four-beat pattern

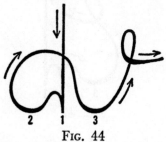

FIG. 44

After one in any beat pattern

FIG. 45

After the last beat in any beat pattern

FIG. 46

After three in the six-beat pattern

FIG. 47

After four in the six-beat pattern

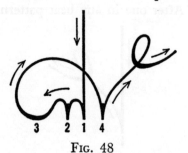

FIG. 48

After five in the six-beat pattern

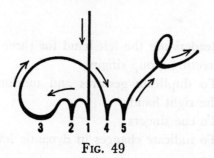

FIG. 49

This gesture for release should be practiced until it looks and feels authoritative and natural. Avoid a floppy sort of wrist and hand appearance, but avoid also a feeling of rigidity. The wrist and forearm should feel supple and free, but very much under control.

49

CHAPTER V

Use of the Left Hand

Song leaders use the left hand for three purposes while directing group singing:
1. To duplicate gestures and motions of the right hand
2. To cue singers
3. To indicate changes in dynamic levels.

Duplicating the Right Hand

When the left hand is used for this purpose, every beat pattern, motion, and gesture given for the right hand in this book will be reversed. They will be executed simultaneously and in the same manner and style as is being done by the right hand, but the direction the left hand moves horizontally will be exactly opposite from that of the right.

The two-beat pattern for the left hand, then, will be as follows:

FIG. 50

The three-beat pattern:

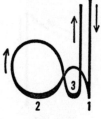

FIG. 51

The four-beat pattern:

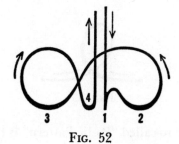

FIG. 52

The six-beat pattern:

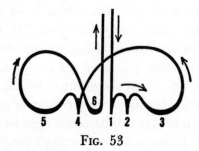

FIG. 53

The preparatory beat:

FIG. 54

The release:

FIG. 55

Note: The so-called "Panic Pattern" is the same for both hands.

The left hand is used for this purpose of duplicating the right hand (1) when there is an unusually large or widespread group to direct, (2) when the song leader is not readily visible by the whole group or the accompanist, (3) when the song is difficult or not well-known, (4) if the group is having difficulty singing together for any of these reasons or others, and (5) it is often used to duplicate the right hand during the first few measures when starting a song to insure a good beginning. Similarly, the left hand might duplicate the right (6) at the beginning and end of subsequent stanzas of the same song to keep the group singing together better. Also, it may be used in this way (7) to emphasize a fermata, accent, release, attack, or change in tempo. The song leader, of course, decides just when the left hand should be used to duplicate the right. Many times this decision must be made on the spur of the moment, and, in fact, it becomes very much an automatic reaction after some experience.

However, unless one or more of the above conditions exist, there is no real reason why the left hand should beat time along with the right. In fact, continuous duplication of the beat patterns without sufficient reason invariably will result in the left hand becoming ineffective in moments when it really is needed. When this happens the singers become so accustomed to continuous motions in both hands that they will not respond to specific gestures that are executed best by the left hand.

Examples of when the left hand might duplicate the right:

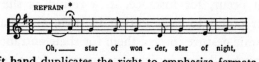

Oh,____ star of won - der, star of night,

(* Left hand duplicates the right to emphasize fermata.)

Fig. 56

53

But it stopp'd short nev-er to go a-gain

(* Left hand emphasizes attack and release.)

FIG. 57

So let the mu-sic play-ay-ay! I'm

(* Left hand emphasizes accents.)
(** Left hand emphasizes fermata.)

FIG. 58

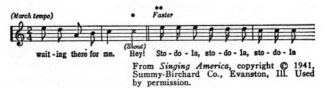

wait-ing there for me. (Shout) Hey! Sto-do-la, sto-do-la, sto-do-la

From *Singing America*, copyright © 1941, Summy-Birchard Co., Evanston, Ill. Used by permission.

(* Left hand emphasizes "Hey!" as a strong accent.)
(** Left hand helps to set faster tempo.)

FIG. 59.

Cueing Singers

Times when the left hand is used to cue singers might occur, for instance, in a round as the song leader points to each section in turn, and makes a rhythmic gesture toward them for their entrance. Or the left hand may indicate an entrance for a moving part, such as in the case of a descant. The left hand also cues sections for antiphonal singing. These cues must be given definitely and rhythmically. And they must be given with a preparatory beat or motion of some sort which will occur on the count *before* the section is to enter. The regular preparatory beat may be used (see page 29), or any other gesture in good taste that is successful in securing everyone's attention for a smooth entrance.

Examples of when the left hand might cue singers:

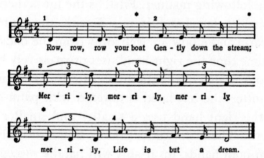

(* Preparatory beat is given here on the count *before* the next section enters.)

FIG. 60

(* Preparatory beat given here to alert descant singers to enter at **.)

FIG. 61

Al - le - lu - ia, le - lu - ia. Joy, joy, joy, Joy, joy,

(* Preparatory beat given here on the count before each section enters.)

FIG. 62

Indicating Dynamic Changes

The left hand is used to indicate dynamic changes in the following manner. First, as the music becomes louder the left hand is raised with the palm *up* (forearm and elbow are well away from the body) ; at the same time the right hand uses progressively larger motions in describing the beat pattern. As the music gets softer, the left hand is lowered with palm *down* and the right hand uses a smaller and smaller beat pattern. These devices, working simultaneously between both hands, invariably will handle successfully crescendos and diminuendos. Sudden changes in dynamics are handled in the same manner except the motions are abrupt. For a suddenly loud effect the left hand is raised quickly to shoulder height, or possibly even higher, with the palm up while the right hand immediately increases the size of the beat pattern. When the music calls for an abrupt change to a softer tone, the left hand is extended to midriff or waist level with palm down while the right hand describes a small beat pattern.

56

Examples of the use of the left hand for changes in dynamics:

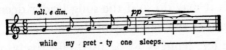

rall. e dim.
pp
while my pret - ty one sleeps.

(* The left hand gradually is lowered with palm down, beginning here, while the right hand decreases the size of the beat pattern.)

FIG. 63

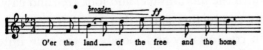

broaden
ff
O'er the land of the free and the home

(* The left hand is raised with palm up, beginning here, while the right hand increases the size of the beat pattern.)

FIG. 64

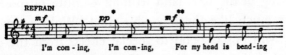

REFRAIN
mf
pp
mf
I'm com - ing, I'm com - ing, For my head is bend - ing

(* Left hand is lowered suddenly, palm down; right hand describes smaller beat pattern.)
(** Left hand is raised suddenly, palm up; right hand describes larger beat pattern.)

FIG. 65

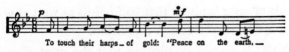

p
mf
To touch their harps of gold: "Peace on the earth.

(* Left hand is raised suddenly, palm up; right hand describes larger beat pattern.)

FIG. 66

When bringing about changes in dynamics the left hand usually will not be duplicating the right hand, although it may do so if the song leader deems it advisable under the exigency of the moment.

If the left hand is to be used effectively, the song leader will need to develop considerable independence between hands. This means that the examples given here and elsewhere should be practiced over and over until the motions feel and look free and easy.

Most conductors agree that the left hand should remain comfortably and loosely at the side unless it actually is being used in one or more of the three ways just described (i.e., duplicating the right, cuing singers, or indicating dynamic changes). Continuous waving of the left hand without definite purpose is very much like the boy who cried "Wolf!"; singers just will not respond to special effects from the left hand if they are accustomed to its senseless waving.

Common faults of beginning song leaders include either using the left hand too much, or not using it at all. Both should be avoided. It must be remembered when learning to use the left hand, as in all the elements of song leading, that bad habits as well as good ones are learned through repetition.

Note: It should be obvious that the most effective song leader is one who knows his songs from memory or at least well enough not to have to hold and watch the songbook, thus releasing both hands for better directing.

Left-Handed Song Leaders

As indicated earlier, all the motions and diagrams in this book are intended for the right-handed person who naturally will beat time with his right hand. However, there is no reason why a left-handed person should not beat time with his left hand. In this case every diagram, horizontal movement, and gesture given herein for the right hand will need to be reversed and applied to the left hand (see pp. 50-52).

By far, the greatest majority of professional conductors beat time with the right hand, and there are some sound reasons for this in addition to just happenstance; but this does not presuppose that songs cannot be led just as effectively with the left hand. Therefore, left-handed song leaders are *not* at a disadvantage, and they should not feel the least bit inferior when it comes to leading group singing.

CHAPTER VI

Special Gestures

Changing Beat Patterns

Although not often encountered, some songs do require changing the beat pattern within the song itself. This may occur in one of several ways. Sometimes the rhythmic scheme will change from measure to measure, and will be so indicated by measure signatures. The young song leader should mark such changes in his own book with heavy pencil or in red so he can perceive at a glance which beat pattern to use. (After some experience this device should not be necessary.)

Example:

Oh, Shen-an-doah, I long to hear you, Way hay, you roll-ing riv-er! Oh, Shen-an-doah, I long to hear you, (etc.)

Fig. 67

Or such changes may not be marked by measure signatures. Most ancient hymns and canticles do not contain measure signatures. Some songs will have a multiple measure signature at the beginning. In either case the song should be studied carefully ahead of time and the changes marked.

Now my wa - gon is full la - den, Full of cross old wo - men. When we pulled up at the mar - ket They all be - gan to quar - rel. Now I do swear that ev - er af - ter I'll take no load of cross old wo - men! Come, horse, get up!

FIG. 68

In songs used for group singing it is more common to find these differences occuring between verse and chorus than within the song itself. Here, too, the change should be marked.

From *Singing America*, copyright © 1941, Summy-Birchard Co., Evanston, Ill. Used by permission.

Fig. 69

The drills on pages 21, 23, and 25 are excellent practice material and will help prepare song leaders to handle those instantaneous changes in beat patterns that sometimes do occur.

Divided Beats

When a song is to be sung very slowly, a "divided" beat pattern often is advisable. This simply gives two impulses *to each beat* in the pattern; it is indicated by rebounding, or bouncing, twice on each count. This second impulse should be smoother and not accented, but is given precisely in exact rhythm. In practicing divided beat patterns (and even when actually directing group singing using a divided beat pattern) the song leader can think or count to himself the familiar "ONE-and, TWO-and," etc., until the motions become graceful, definite, and natural.

Examples:

DIVIDED TWO-BEAT

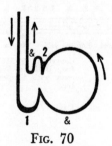

Fig. 70

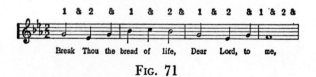

Break Thou the bread of life, Dear Lord, to me,

Fig. 71

63

Swing Low, Sweet Char - i - ot, ___ Com - in' for to car - ry me home!

From *All-American Song Book*. Used by permission of The Big 3 Music Corporation.

Fig. 72

DIVIDED THREE-BEAT

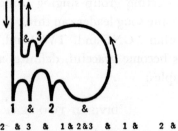

Kum ba yah, my Lord, Kum ba yah! Kum ba yah, my Lord, Kum ba (etc.)

Copyright © MCMLVII, Shawnee Press, Inc., Delaware Water Gap, Pa., by arrangement with Cooperative Recreation Service, Inc.

Fig. 73

DIVIDED FOUR-BEAT

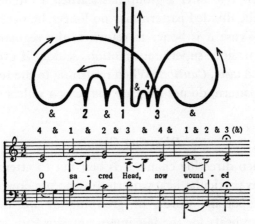

FIG. 74

DIVIDED SIX-BEAT

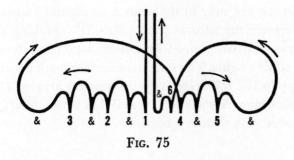

FIG. 75

The divided six-beat is not commonly found.
A song leader will need to decide just when the

divided beat pattern should be used. Also, it is quite possible that after a group has learned a rather slow song the divided pattern may no longer be necessary; in this case it is better to return to the regular beat pattern, since superfluous motions seldom if ever are in good taste. *Caution:* When returning to the regular beat pattern, do not increase the tempo unless called for.

Directing Chants

When directing chants it is best not to attempt to use any particular beat pattern. Instead use downbeats for important words, or grouping of words, and smaller beats for the less important words or groupings. These smaller beats will be similar to the secondary rebounds in divided beat patterns.

Words in a chant naturally fall into groups and properly are sung in the manner of dignified speech. Wherever the natural stress falls while speaking the phrases will determine where the musical stress should be while singing. The song leader might mark his own copy in the following way, the vertical arrows (↓) indicating a strong downbeat and the curved lines (◡) weaker (but definite) beats:

Example:

FIG. 76

CHAPTER VII

Additional Characteristics of Outstanding Song Leaders

Developing Expressive Conducting

The ability to lead songs expressively comes after much practice in private and actual experience before a group. However, there are several things which will hasten this learning period and should be borne in mind.

Loud songs demand large beat patterns; soft songs require smaller patterns. A rhythmic song calls for more rebound, or bounce; a sustained and quiet song needs less rebound and a smoother pattern.

Once the beat patterns have been mastered, the prospective song leader should sing aloud (lightly and easily) the songs he would direct; he should breathe when the group would breathe and try to experience the song emotionally in the same manner he would expect from his group. That is, he should feel deep sincerity of thought and purpose if the song calls for it, or joviality, or religious conviction, or lightheartedness, or whatever the words and mood of the music suggest.

If the song leader sings aloud while directing a group, he should sing with enthusiasm but not loudly.

Continuous loud singing by the leader detracts from the response he desires from the group. Although at times the leader may have to sing lustily, it should be only momentary, and he should resort to it only when necessary. Loud singing calls attention to the leader himself, and, while admittedly he is all-important for a successful song session, his importance should not be obvious and noticeably forced upon the group. Likewise, often it is much better not to sing at all or to restrict singing to such times as the beginnings of stanzas and choruses or to changes in tempo or rhythm. Again, experience and the dictates of the moment will determine the need and advisability of whether or not to sing with the group, and the song leader will react in this respect almost automatically.

The successful song leader who directs expressively keeps his eyes and thoughts constantly ahead of what the group is singing. He is at least a measure ahead in his thinking. That way he never reaches a place where he might be thrown off-guard because of a fermata, change in beat pattern, accents, and the like. Then he not only is ready himself for whatever comes next, but he prepares his group somewhat in advance by the style of his directing. The group really is hardly aware of this anticipatory element in the song session; they just subconsciously feel secure in whatever they may be singing.

To develop expressive directing, review **Chap. II.** Do not forget to practice directing in front of a mirror. Strive constantly to improve posture, graceful motions, pleasant facial expressions, and style. Keep away from fancy flourishes, but do not lapse into a timid or mousy style. More often than not—particularly in early stages—the happy medium will be the best.

Inspiration and Artistry

After the basic fundamentals have been mastered and some degree of confidence has been acquired, and after a song leader has learned to direct songs expressively, the extra qualities of inspiration and artistry become extremely important. These cannot be taught in the usual pedagogical sense, and they differ immensely between individuals. They emerge from such intangible qualities as depth of understanding, breadth of living, emotional maturity, adaptability to changing moods and emotions, and yes, even dramaticism to some extent. This latter must not be confused with a cheap type of showmanship. (A sense of the appropriateness of true showmanship is not bad within itself; it should be avoided, though, when it begins to dominate the spirit of the occasion. Therein lies the danger.)

Perhaps the one thing which will inspire a group more than anything else is the enthusiasm of the song leader. This does not mean that technical perfection of time-beating or a mastery of the mechanical details of musicianship are unimportant—not at all. It simply means that enthusiasm is a "must" for a song leader. In fact (and musicians many times do not like to admit this) some of the most effective song leaders actually have great inadequacy in pure musical techniques. But the warmth of their personalities, their genuine love of what is true, good, and beautiful, their pleasant smiles, their winning ways with a group—all these factors combine to make people want to respond to them.

Now, when these factors are combined with a solid foundation of musical study, there literally are no limits to the success of such a a song leader.

Remember that a smile is contagious! This doesn't imply an artificial "light-bulb" sort of thing that can be turned on and off at will. Instead, it means that cheerfulness (even when something goes wrong during a song session) is without a substitute. Learn to laugh *with* the group, but never *at* them.

Your own sensitivity for what is good, true, and beautiful will tend to evoke the same from your group. They not only consciously or subconsciously want to reflect the leader's enthusiasm and ready smile, they also want to reflect his capacities for pure musical enjoyment and appreciation for the opportunities at hand.

Fortunately, radio, television, hi-fi and stereo phonographs in recent years have stimulated an immensely healthy interest in music in general. The fact that people hear good music and want good music without a doubt increases their capacity for responding to leadership that is inspired itself and seeks to inspire others. Further, our schools, churches, and community groups are offering more and better music for both singers and listeners than ever before. Business, industry, and professions are utilizing music more and more in a variety of ways. All this serves to raise musical standards and tastes, and, therefore, the readiness to respond is more apparent when moments of inspiration are presented by an inspired song leader.

Along with this increase in discerning musical tastes and experiences comes a very real challenge. Groups no longer are content with second-rate musical leadership even in the matter of group singing. Unless real dynamic leadership that inspires a group to respond heartily is apparent, one of three conditions will likely occur: a general apathetic atmosphere will settle over the group with no real response, a few brave persons will try halfheartedly to sing, or open discourtesy will develop with matters soon getting out of hand. None of these situations need come about. The remedy lies in an enthusiastic and alert song leader who is well-prepared, expressive, inspiring, and artistic.

In the matter of artistry, song leading differs from other conducting techniques. A skilled song leader does not strive for perfection of rendition as does the symphonic or choral conductor. The latter drills his players or singers for hours on mechanical details, delicate nuances, style, rubatos, and the like. The artistic perfection the song leader strives for lies in the response he seeks from his singers who may or may not be musicians in the usual sense. This response may be in the form of personal and group excitement; of stimulating the emotions; of finding common expression through common means without a display of technical skills; the pure joy of group concentration on beauty for the sake of beauty alone—as is the case when many voices are raised together with no thought of proper phrasing or breath control or tone production but just to "make it sound pretty"; to have some side-splitting laughter from fun and action songs; or to voice commitment and/or reaffirm some grand ideas. These are some of the areas of artistic expression with which song leaders are concerned.

To develop this artistry, an aspiring song leader should observe other leaders as often as possible in every conceivable situation. This will be beneficial in several ways: he will learn both what to do and what not to do to achieve results; he will learn devices and shortcuts; and he will learn new methods and ways and means. By critically observing other song leaders he will begin instinctively to experience elation or disappointment along with the person who is leading; his own sense of artistry is bound to be stirred when he no longer is just a casual participant but is experiencing every motion, gesture, and word of encouragement along with the leader.

Also, artistry will develop with experience in actually leading songs before a group (provided, of course, there is also personal depth of understanding and breadth of emotional development in the leader to begin with). Once you have learned the beat patterns, *never* refuse to lead songs. There is no teacher quite as effective and thorough as experience. Too, it is a fact that once you have refused to lead songs because of insecurity and fear, it will only be more difficult when (and *if*) the opportunity comes again. The first few times you stand before a group you may feel very inadequate, nervous, and insecure. As a rule it is best that you not let the group know you feel this way, since the more confidence they have in you the better they will respond. On the other hand, it is conceivable that acknowledging one's own inexperience in a lighthearted and offhanded manner may serve to break the ice and put you at ease, but it is doubtful that any real purpose would be served by such an admission.

74

Then at every opportunity listen to good music of every imaginable style—classic, popular, folk—anything that can be considered to be in good taste. Practice beating time while you are listening, using the appropriate gestures. Remember that soft, dreamy, and flowing music calls for rather small and smooth gestures; loud and rhythmic music demands more vigorous motions.

Finally, strive always to increase your own understanding and enjoyment of music for its own sake as an art. Art for art's sake is not to be sneered at. The more you know about music, as with any of the arts, the greater will be your own capacity for responding to artistry itself and for invoking this response from others. Therefore, your own efforts to enrich the musical experiences of persons through group singing will be greatly enhanced.

Since the very dawn of man's awareness that he is set apart from the other wonders of creation with a mind, a will, emotions, a spirit, and a conscience, he has used artistic means to express and record not only concrete events that happen but also his hopes, fears, elations, disappointments, and faith in a Power beyond his own. This yen for artistic expression has arisen through the centuries as almost a necessity of life itself along with the needs of food, shelter, and the like. Music, of course, has not been the least among these avenues of expression, and today it still

perhaps is more universally experienced than any of
the other means of emotional release. Artistry is not
to be taken lightly, then, in group singing. However,
it cannot be "taught" in the usual sense of the word;
it must be "caught" and nurtured and fed and en-
couraged and drawn out in any and every possible
way. Ultimate perfection and absolute satisfaction
must be striven for, but the wise and mature song
leader acknowledges it always as just a little beyond
his grasp. Perhaps the song leader feels he comes
closest to this realization when, after a song session is
over, people cluster around him with eyes dancing
and demanding more.

CHAPTER VIII

General Suggestions

Planning Ahead

The wise song leader will plan his song sessions carefully ahead of time; this is important. He never is at a loss as to what to sing or what to say. He never frantically thumbs through a book at the last moment looking for something to sing.

When planning these song sessions do so with such things in mind as the specific occasion at hand, the size of the group, the time of day, surroundings, season of the year, age group, what has preceded and what will follow the session, whether or not a piano will be used, and anything else that might effect the time for singing.

The Accompaniment

Directors, be considerate of the accompanist. Realize that some pianists just cannot sight-read well, or transpose easily, or adapt to sudden changes. Whenever possible, check with the pianist ahead of time to make certain he can play the songs and if he can transpose (if this is desirable). Also, point out any changes in a song or deviations you might call for. Give him a list of the songs you intend to use. Discuss song introductions and decide whether to use a single chord, a phrase, or a single tone. Check on the position of the piano; make certain the pianist can see you easily. Do not embarrass your pianist! This not only is impolite and in poor taste, but you may have difficulty finding another pianist for another song session! Remember that your pianist really can make or break the song session. Friendliness and courtesy are all-important in this relationship as in all personal contacts. Accompanists like to feel secure and know what will happen next.

Pianists, remember you are not the director, even though you may be perfectly capable of leading a song session yourself. Therefore, you must permit the song leader to lead the songs as he wishes with regard to tempos, dynamics, artistic deviations, etc.

Know how to play the songs that will be called for —this is your responsibility! Practice them ahead of time if necessary. If you do not know the music, or have a copy of it, make *every* effort to obtain one. Be available ahead of time for consultation with the director; don't hesitate to ask what he intends to use in the song session if he neglects to seek you out first with this information. If you are accompanying for a director for the first time, find out what he prefers for an introduction—chord, first phrase, last phrase, single tone.

As introductory material it is effective to be able

to end on the dominant chord $(V$ or $V_7)$ after playing a familiar fragment from any song called for; this gives an "onward" feeling and makes for an easy entrance by the group. Practice will facilitate this device.

"Lily-fingered" playing seldom if ever is effective for group singing. A firm touch is important; actual volume will depend upon the size of the group, style of the song, position of the piano, size and resonance of the room, and resonance of the piano itself. Avoid playing lopsided chords (broken chords); this does not give a feeling of security and solidity. Play the songs as written, except it is permissible and effective at times to play single bass notes as octaves, or even play them an octave lower for added strength. Likewise, the right hand can be raised an octave at times if by doing so the overall effect is kept in good taste; beware that doing this does not result in a cheap and tin-pan accompaniment. While some songs may be enhanced by elaborating on the basic harmonic structure, too much of this is not effective and actually becomes tiresome. Keep it all within the bounds of good taste.

Look ahead at what comes next and be ready for it. It is disconcerting to the group and the director if the pianist is not ready for the next song. If there is a lag in time while the pianist hunts for a book or page number, or has to adjust the bench, or some other thing, the effect of a spirited and exciting song session is in danger of being destroyed.

Check on the position of the piano ahead of time so you can see the director easily—then, watch him! Adjust the bench, open the piano lid, check the pedals, and key-action, and do any number of other things ahead of time; during the song session is no time for these things.

Do not play—even softly—while the director is talking to the group. This is annoying to both the leader and the group.

Learn to sight-read and transpose. These two abilities cannot be overemphasized.

Learn many, many songs by memory in comfortable keys. Many fine songs cannot be sung easily by most people because of the keys in which they are written.

Introducing New Songs

New songs, and new ways of singing old songs, should be introduced regularly to a group which sings together frequently. However, this can be overdone; new songs should not be presented so often that the whole idea becomes boring. When properly spaced, the introduction of something new will be refreshing and interesting. After a new song has been learned, it should be scheduled in several consecutive song sessions that follow, and then used more or less irregularly as a part of the entire repertory.

A simple and short explanation of a new song may be desirable, but these remarks should be kept at a minimum. Explanatory words should be limited to such things as origin, intended use, interesting facts about the song itself, including the author and composer, or, they should be omitted altogether.

The director needs to know the new song very well himself before he attempts to teach it to others; this is true for the accompanist, also. In fact, a new song is taught easier if the song leader has it memorized. Many new songs can be grasped easier and faster if they are taught by the rote method.

Teaching Songs by Rote

1. Leader sings entire song (clearly and with simple interpretation).
   a) Rote songs are taught more easily without the use of piano, especially in the case of younger children.
2. Leader may discuss the song—origin, words, mood, message, etc.
   a) This step is optional and may be omitted.
3. Leader sings first phrase—group sings first phrase.
   a) Leader hums pitch of beginning note for group before they answer; or preferably, leader intones "Ready, Sing!" on the proper pitch and in correct rhythm.
4. Leader repeats Step Three for each phrase of song.
   a) In longer and more difficult songs, after each phrase has been repeated the leader may com-

81

bine two phrases, singing as in Step Three, and the group answering. Or phrases may be combined from the very first if the group is alert and the phrases are not too difficult.

5. After all phrases have been taught, the leader may wish to isolate and repeat difficult phrase (s) slowly, with the group answering.

   a) This step may not be necessary and is therefore optional.

6. Leader sings entire song through again—group sings entire song (with piano accompaniment, if desired) .

Note: Teaching rote songs will be simplified if the leader will adopt the habit of intoning "Ready, Sing!" *in the rhythm and tempo* as well as on the *proper pitch* of the phrase. A little practice will make this device easy and habitual.

The above steps in teaching rote songs are to be used only as a guide by prospective song leaders. Different groups may require varying approaches depending on age, difficulty and style of the song, experience of the group, and experience of the leader.

When introducing new songs, sometimes it is best not to use a regular beat pattern. Instead simply indicate changing pitch levels of the notes by rhythmically raising or lowering the hand as each note or group of notes is sung. Thus, as an illustration, "Three Blind Mice" would be indicated as follows:

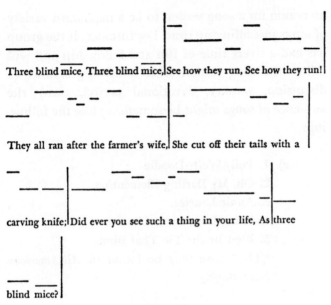

Three blind mice, Three blind mice, See how they run, See how they run!

They all ran after the farmer's wife, She cut off their tails with a

carving knife; Did ever you see such a thing in your life, As three

blind mice?

FIG. 77

(Hand position for above device: palm down, horizontal across body. ——— indicates relative positions of hand for each note, or group of notes.) This is an effective device, and a little practice makes it easy to use. After a new song has been learned, the regular beat pattern should be used.

Planning the Song Session

The best song sessions are those that move logically from what has preceded to what will follow. There is no reason for a song session to be a haphazard variety of songs just filling up time. For instance, if the group has had a lively time of fun and fellowship and will follow the song session with something serious (a discussion, speaker, devotional period, class) the sequence of songs might be something like the following:

a) 1. Polly-Wolly-Doodle
   2. Oh, My Darling Clementine
   3. Annie Laurie
   4. Swing Low, Sweet Chariot
   5. Blest Be the Tie That Binds
   (The above may be found in *All-American Song Book*.)

b) 1. Let Us Sing Together
   2. Waltzing Matilda
   3. Holla Hi, Holla Ho
   4. Let Us Break Bread Together
   5. Spirit of the Living God
   (The above may be found in *Sing It Again*.)

If the group has just finished a serious period and will move into a fun session, the order of the sequence of songs listed in either (*a*) or (*b*) will simply be reversed.

The alert song leader will know lots of songs; he

84

may have his own scrapbooks of songs gathered from many sources far and wide in addition to standard collections that are generally available. He will be ready for a song session at just any time. And, interestingly, sometimes the best leadership in group singing comes from someone not directing but who knows many songs and has the courage to lead out on them; at times it is far better not to stand before the group waving the arms, but to sit in the group having song after song ready to start as each is finished.

Many times persons will call out the names of songs they would like to have sung. This is acceptable provided the group is small and informal and provided the pianist knows the songs being called for and can play them. However, this sort of thing can degenerate very easily into a free-for-all yelling time between songs. It is far better to plan carefully the entire song session; if someone asks for a particular song, and the time does not seem proper for it, the song leader kindly but firmly says, "We'll save that one for next time," and he says it with a smile!

Do's and Don'ts

Do

Be pleasant, always. There is no substitute for a smile and genuine likability. Cultivate the latter.

Show your best personality. Accept success or difficulty

85

graciously and gracefully. Go out of your way to be nice to people.

Use songs of the highest order. New twists to old songs are fun, but make certain you do so with songs that cannot offend. There are so very many fine songs to sing there is no reason why questionable songs ever should be sung.

Watch the range of songs—some may need transposing.

Plan your song session ahead of time, and don't forget to check with your pianist ahead of time.

Show confidence; be assertive in your position of leadership.

Direct plainly and positively.

Cultivate qualities of inspiration, expressiveness, and artistry.

Remember: enthusiasm and smiles are contagious; use them often.

Don't

Be grumpy, irritated, bored, cocky, or conceited. And don't let little things that may go wrong bother you; be bigger than your problems.

Use songs with questionable words (off-color, making fun of speech, nationality, religion, etc.), or inferior music (poor melody, weak harmony and rhythm, etc.). Do not burlesque spirituals and folk songs; most racial and cultural groups are justly proud of their musical heritage, and it is in poor taste to use folk songs as nonsense songs unless they are written as such.

Turn the song session into a yell session or free-for-all.

Fumble for what to sing or say next, or waste time, or carry on private conversations with persons in the group.

Direct wildly as though you were catching flies, or mousy-like as though you were afraid someone would see you—let your directing reflect the spirit of the music.

Refuse to lead group singing, ever! Your opportunity may never come again (and, your leading a song session may open up entirely new fields for you!).

Talk too much. "Sing more and talk less" is a good rule for song leaders.

Be a sourpuss and/or satisfied with your accomplishments; there are always more things to learn and more goals to reach.

Recapitulation. After all is said and done, the opening statement of this book still holds true: Anyone with a sense of rhythm can learn to lead group singing!

Appendix I
Sources of Material

The following is a partial list of books containing songs which are suitable for group singing. Many may be examined at local music stores. Most successful song leaders have several of these books in their personal music libraries. Leaders also make up their own private collections of songs and parodies which are gathered through the years from many sources.

All-American Song Book, compiled and edited by Dr. Joseph E. Maddy and Dr. Otto Miessner. Robbins Music Corp. (An excellent collection of over 150 standard and popular standard favorites.)

American Airs, compiled and arranged by George L. Leaman. Edwin H. Morris & Co., Inc. (68 songs; includes some college, military, folk, and standard favorites.)

American Folk Song Series, G. Schirmer. (20 sets; includes all types of American folk songs.)

Americana Collection, compiled, arranged, and edited by Arthur H. Brandenburg, *et al.* Rubank, Inc. (Contains 76 standard favorites.)

Canciones Panamericanas, Silver Burdett Co. (28 representative songs from Latin America and North America.)

Christmas in Song, compiled and arranged by Theo. Preuss. Rubank, Inc. (Excellent collection of types and styles of carols, noels, hymns of praise and worship, and merry songs.)

Cowboy Sings, The, edited by Kenneth S. Clark. Paull-Pioneer Music Corp. (Contains 79 songs of the West.)

Golden Book of Favorite Songs, The, Hall and Mc-Creary Co. (Fine collection of about 200 standard favorites.)

Everyday Song Book, The, Cable Co. (Unique song book graded in five parts for use with little children up through youth; instructions and suggestions from music education standpoint on the young voice and how best to use the songs included.)

Get-Together Songs, edited by Ellen Jane Lorenz and Harry C. Eldridge. Lorenz Publishing Co. (Contains 246 standard and not so well-known songs of every type for group singing; topical index is useful.)

Home and Community Song Book, The, E. C. Schirmer Music Co. (Contains over 100 songs for general singing but without the usual rounds and action songs.)

Keep On Singing, edited by Kenneth S. Clark. Paull-Pioneer Music Corp. (Over 100 excellent songs of high calibre, but some are not well-known.)

Legion Airs, compiled and edited by Frank E. Peat

and Lee O. Smith. Leo Feist, Inc. (A collection of both well-known and unfamiliar songs of the military.)

Let Voices Ring, compiled and arranged by Ruth Heller and Walter Goodell. Hall & McCreary Co. (Excellent collection for youth and adults of 109 secular songs of all types.)

Lonesome Tunes from the Mountains of Kentucky, H. W. Gray Co. (A widely used and popular collection of mountain songs.)

New American Song Book, The, edited by Oberndorfer, *et al.* Hall & McCreary Co. (Collection of standard songs of America from Colonial days to the present; topical type index is useful; explanatory comments on songs from various periods.)

Songs for Every Purpose and Occasion, Hall & McCreary Co. (Large collection of familiar songs from various countries.)

Songs We Sing, edited by Fowler Smith, *et al.* Hall & McCreary Co. (Contains many old favorites and a number of less familiar songs.)

United We Sing, arranged by D. M. Burton. Edwin H. Morris & Co. (Collection of patriotic songs and songs popular with the military.)

The following is a partial list of pocket-size song books that are popular across the nation particularly with youth groups. They generally contain folk songs of various countries, rounds, and some hymns and spirituals. Each book contains some songs not found in other similar volumes. Many songs have only the words and melody line printed, but some do have chords indicated for the pianist; a few songs will have both the treble and bass parts written out. These are excellent books. They are economically priced, and because of their compact size are easily transported and handled both in small and large groups. Most of these books are published by Cooperative Recreation Service, Delaware, Ohio, but may be ordered also from the other sources listed.

A Little Carol Book (Christmas carols), Cooperative Recreation Service, Delaware, Ohio.

Let Us Sing Together, Methodist Board of Education, 1801 6th Avenue, North, Birmingham, Ala.

Lift Every Voice, The Service Department, Box 871, Nashville, Tenn.

Of Joy and Praise, Youth Department, North Georgia Conference, Methodist Board of Education, 407 Wesley Memorial Building, 63 Auburn Avenue, Atlanta 3, Ga.

Rejoice and Sing, Cooperative Song Service. (Published for the Youth Fellowships of The Cumberland Presbyterian Church, The Presbyterian Church, U. S., the United Presbyterian Church, U.S.A., and The Reformed Church in America.)

Romancing, Cooperative Recreation Service. (Contains folk type love songs along with games and proverbs.)

Sing a Tune, Cooperative Song Service. (Compiled by a committee sponsored by The Committee on Children's Work and The Committee on Camps and Conferences, Division of Christian Education of the National Council of Churches.)

Sing for the Fun of It, Florida MYF, Box 78, Lakeland, Fla.

Sing It Again, The Service Department, Box 871, Nashville, Tenn.

Song in the Air (Christmas carols), The Service Department, Box 871, Nashville, Tenn.

The following books are recommended for study and reference purposes.

Bakaleinikoff, V. *Elementary Rules of Conducting.* New York: Belwin, Inc., 1938.

Davison, Archibald T. *Choral Conducting.* Cambridge: Harvard University Press, 1940.

Green, Elizabeth A. H. *The Modern Conductor.* Englewood Cliffs, N. J.: Prentice-Hall, 1961.

Rice, William C. *Basic Principles of Singing,* Abingdon Press, 1961.

Rudolf, Max. *The Grammar of Conducting.* New York: G. Schirmer, Inc., 1950.

Scherchen, H., *Handbook of Conducting.* London: Oxford Press, 1933.

Sydnor, James R. *The Training of Church Choirs,* Abingdon Press, 1963.

Van Hoesen, K. *Handbook of Conducting.* New York: Appleton-Century-Crofts, Inc., 1950.

Wilson, H. R. *Lead a Song!* Minneapolis: Hall and McCreary Co., 1942.

Appendix II

Other Beat Patterns

Songs commonly used in group singing may be directed using the two-beat, three-beat (or one), four-beat, and six-beat patterns. The following beat patterns are included for reference and practice purposes only.

THE FIVE-BEAT PATTERN

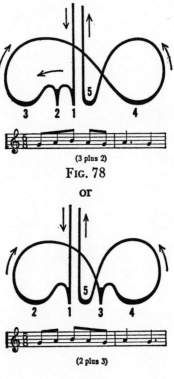

(3 plus 2)

Fig. 78

or

(2 plus 3)

Fig. 79

Note: Fast tempi in "five" may be conducted better as uneven *two* beats in the measures. The grouping of notes which determine where the secondary accents occur will dictate whether the first beat will be short and the second long, or vice versa.

THE SEVEN-BEAT PATTERN

(3 plus 2 plus 2)

Fig. 80

or

(2 plus 2 plus 3)

Fig. 81

or

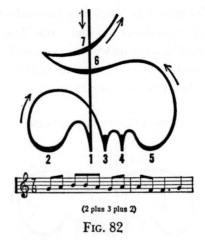

(2 plus 3 plus 2)

FIG. 82

Note: Fast tempi in "seven" may be conducted using uneven *three*-beat patterns.

THE EIGHT-BEAT PATTERN

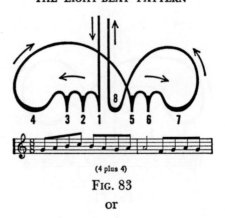

(4 plus 4)

FIG. 83

or

96

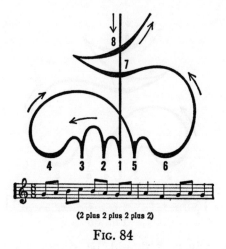

(2 plus 2 plus 2 plus 2)

FIG. 84

THE NINE-BEAT PATTERN

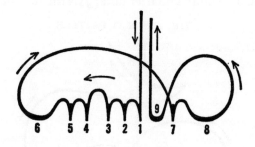

or
(optional)

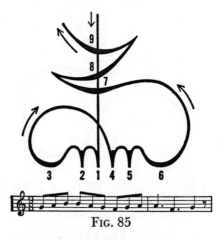

FIG. 85

Note: Lively $\frac{9}{8}$ should be conducted using the three-beat pattern, the second beat occurring on count four of the measure and the third beat on count seven. The dotted quarter note ($\,\!\,$) is the unit of value.

THE TEN-BEAT PATTERN

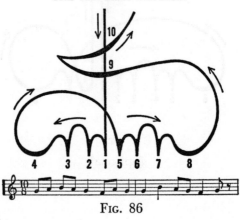

FIG. 86

THE ELEVEN-BEAT PATTERN

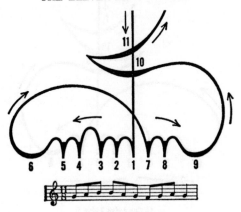

(3 plus 3 plus 3 plus 2)

FIG. 87

or

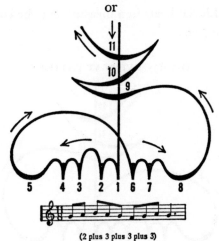

(2 plus 3 plus 3 plus 3)

FIG. 88

or

99

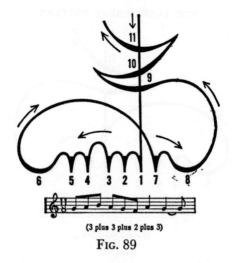

(3 plus 3 plus 2 plus 3)

Fig. 89

Note: Eleven beats in a measure may be conducted in uneven *four*.

THE TWELVE-BEAT PATTERN

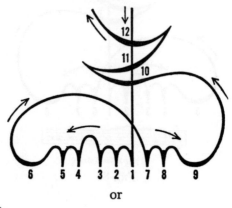

or

100

(optional)

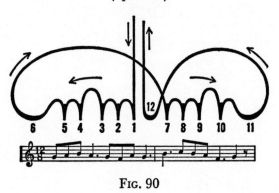

FIG. 90

Note: Lively $\frac{12}{8}$ should be conducted using the *four-*beat pattern, the second beat occurring on count four of the measure, the third beat on count seven and the fourth beat on count ten. The dotted quarter note (♩.) is the unit of value.

(optional)

Meter 1:

Meter 1: 4/4 should be conducted using the four-beat pattern: the second beat occurring on countdown... of the measure, the third beat on count seven and the fourth beat on count nine. The dotted quarter note (♩.) is the unit of value.

INDEX OF SONGS
AND MUSICAL EXAMPLES

GENERAL INDEX